Notes from the Field

Robert P. Caldwell, Jr., M.A.

Notes from the Field

20 years of coaching family business

"Son, you're a better man than I." These were the last words my father spoke to me shortly before his death over 20 years ago. It was near sunset on a December evening shortly before Christmas. I'd been sitting with him as I had been doing for the past few weeks of his final illness and was getting ready to go home to my family.

We were alone in his big bedroom when I leaned over his bed and kissed his unshaven cheek. "Dad, you're a wonderful man," I said. Much to my surprise, he looked up at me and in a strong voice, unlike anything I'd heard from him in weeks, said those fateful words.

Soon thereafter Dad died and our 15 years of working together ended. But the residue of those years have stayed with me and grown in value more than 2 decades later. That time together laid the foundation of the work I've done since with many family business owners and members.

What you're about to read is a collection of articles written for a number of newspapers, newsletters and presentations during my 20+ year sojourn into the world of family, money, business and emotion. The wisdom of this collection is acquired from my time with my father, my mentor Arno Hart and the great people with whom I've worked.

For over 40 years I've kept a journal. Into these 90+ stenographer pads I've poured my reflections and experiences with Dad, Arno and many others who form the basis of the content of this collection. I've been an interested observer while also being a sometimes willing, sometimes unwilling participant.

At times working with family is a great blessing, at others a dark curse. Whether you own, are heir to, or work for a family business or business partnership, you may find some insight into the subtle interplay of emotion, personality and turmoil that seems an inevitable part of that work together.

My goal is not to let this wisdom be wasted and to spread it to those who want to find another way.

Table of Contents

NOTES FROM THE FIELD 7

ACKNOWLEDGMENTS 8

Stand Up and Be Counted in Your Family Business 10

The Tripping Point 14

The Comb Over Effect 18

Tell Me a Story 21

The Get Rich and Stay Rich Equation 24

The Fifth Child 27

Change and Hope 30

COMMUNICATION AND RELATIONSHIP **34**

The Paradox of Business Partner Relationships 35

Six Things I Know About My Family Business 38

The Human Side of Wealth Transfer 41

The Secrecy Time Bomb 44

Home for the Holidays: 47

Don't Be Defined by the Pressures of the Time 50

"If something happens to me. . ." 53

**LEADERSHIP, GOVERNANCE AND
MANAGEMENT** **56**

Three Keys for Developing Worthy Successors 57

Three Possibilities of Family Business 60

Family Business during Difficult Times: leadership, passion and education.. 62

Adding Value to All Our Customers 66

Ordinary People, Extraordinary Results............................ 70

Four Critical Aspects of Family Business 73

The Halloween Workplace... 78

ABOUT THE AUTHOR...81

NOTES FROM THE FIELD

ACKNOWLEDGMENTS

I did my work for my M.A. thesis in the days before there was an internet full of data. My research happened in the stacks of UNC-Asheville and the archives of the Family Firm Institute. Other research was done by meeting some of the stars in the universe of family business consulting. John Ward, Gerry LeVan, Leonard Danco, Ron Reece, Stan Mandel and John Goss come to mind from their writing and from many private conversations.

These articles been written over a 20 year period and from the inspiration of many great writers, thinkers and clients. I owe a debt of gratitude to those who have provided me their time and their talents and I'm very grateful I learned to listen to and observe those who taught me to be a lifelong learner.

If I have used something you wrote, that I found important and put it in my notes over all these years, please let me know and I will gladly give you the deserved credit. What you wrote, and I have incorporated here, is valuable information. It's valuable for a lot of family and non-family members who work together. It is this type of wisdom I want to share and pass along.

Family business is the backbone of the world's economy. I want to give it all the help I can find!

Stand Up and Be Counted in Your Family Business

A great paradox of life is that we sometimes find it so hard to talk about intimate things with family members, yet, when we fly for three hours next to a total stranger we're likely to walk off the airplane knowing each other's detailed life history. Sometimes it's easier to vent real feelings on someone you'll most likely never see again, than with a family member we fear will construe heartfelt expressions of feeling as weakness, and use it to our detriment.

While it may seem risky in the beginning, the effect of honest communication in the family business is awe-inspiring. It often contributes to the breaking down of old barriers, just as the Iron Curtain fell partially because of the radical advancement of communications technology; new ideas could no longer be kept from people. Communication helps create a firm foundation for any business to survive and thrive.

Hard feelings and distrust among family members may go back decades. Instead of dealing with current situations while looking through the lens of the past, it's helpful to keep reminding oneself that age and maturity can have a softening effect if we let it. Sibling rivalry and jealousy can often be traced back to infancy. Parents' judgment of an adult child may date back to a teenage indiscretion. Generally speaking, people act in accordance with the way they're treated. If I'm treated as incompetent by a parent, then chances are that's the way I'll behave in their presence.

One thing that led to my interest in dealing with family business was the observation of how we adult children of entrepreneurs continue to act fearfully and inauthentically with our parents. As James Hillman, the Jungian analyst and author once said, "We go home for the holidays as 45-year old men, but when we reach for the doorbell we become 10-year old boys again." The only thing that precludes us from feeling mature and equal with our parents is our unwillingness or inability to perceive ourselves as such.

If you're willing and able to stand up for yourself vis-à-vis the parent with whom you have difficulty, at some point that parent will usually recognize that you're an adult. It's important that every adult child in a family business situation learns to express him or herself honestly, otherwise the foundation of the business begins to decay and its stability is threatened.

This change in behavior isn't just about being nice or using the business as a platform for therapy, but rather a bottom line fact of life in a company. If I'm to be the successor, or if any aspect of the enterprise is to eventually be put in my charge, I had better feel capable and competent enough to manage it. If I'm hobbled by anxiety and fear that I don't measure up, there's a good likelihood I won't.

Years ago when my father and I started to work together, I got so frustrated by what I felt were his irrational demands and controlling methods I was ready to quit. My mentor friend, Arno Hart, said he wanted me to talk to someone before I did that. He took me to visit Carlyle Marney, the renowned theologian and pastoral counselor. After hearing my story, Marney stared at me with his hawk -gaze and said, "When you came here, I didn't think you could continue working with your father, but now I think you can, but there are two things you have to do: First, you have to remain who you are and secondly, you have to come alongside this man as an equal."

I didn't want to leave the business, because I knew the value of our potential working relationship, but I couldn't take it any longer the way it was. Ironically, it was not knowing what else to do or where else to turn that allowed me to hear what Marney had to say and to begin to act on it.

I began telling my father the truth about how I felt. I began to get more vocal. By doing that which I thought would endanger our relationship, standing up for myself and trying to see him as my equal, our relationship began to improve. Dad saw I was a stronger person than he had believed, and he saw that perhaps I did have the grit to succeed him as chief executive. We both began to realize that our real business was to become mutually supportive partners in this enterprise that had provided such a good livelihood to so many people.

My father died, our industry underwent rapid change, and I sold the business, but I'm convinced that by acting on Marney's suggestion 20 years ago I became much better prepared to handle the subsequent challenges I've faced.

We in family business are fortunate. We have the opportunity to face up to areas of our life that need development and to deal with them in an atmosphere where some degree of love and support exist. We work in environments in which, hopefully, content is valued more than form. More often than not in Corporate America, standing up and expressing oneself honestly is at best discouraged and at worst professional suicide. In those hallowed halls, the continuation of the business depends less on personal content and more on structural form.

Adult children in family business can begin to act as adults, to stand up and be counted by having the fortitude to overcome their childhood conditioning. Parents can begin to encourage their adult children who are in the business to express themselves more fully and directly by asking for, and listening to, their opinions. This simple act also encourages younger family members to begin thinking in terms of what is best for the business. After all, if they are going to be listened to, they'd better have something worthwhile to say.

Gratifying results can occur when even small steps toward change are taken. Though it isn't easy and it may be frightening, and everyone involved may need to find some appropriate support, the fruits of this work are particularly sweet for both the family and the business.

The Tripping Point

Malcolm Gladwell introduced us to the concept of "The Tipping Point" in his 2000 book. He defines a *tipping point as the* "the level at which the momentum for change becomes unstoppable." We've all lately seen vivid examples of when a tipping point has been reached: the demise of Wachovia—who'd have thought that was a probability just a few years ago?! The death of the house that Madoff built, unfortunately as a house of cards, also met the unstoppable momentum for change. And 9/11, the defining moment of our generation, a time when the flattening of the world was consummated, is another example of the momentum of change. Such are but a few stark examples of the inevitability of change and the inability of anyone or anything to alter or deflect it away.

There's another point I use with family business clients that I call the "tripping point." Animosities and jealousies have been swept under the rug for so long the lump can no longer just be stepped over and ignored; it's so big now it will trip you up.

Working with a client a few week s ago, I watched and facilitated while two couples, related by blood and property decided the time had come to no longer jointly own an inherited piece of real estate. It is a large lot with an historic old house on a beautiful lake. One brother loved the house and lot for the sentimental value it holds for him and his family. The other brother lives there and needed to use the property for income generation. They were at an impasse and turned to me to help them sort it out.

As is often the case, the spouses have a tremendous influence on the outcome of these mediations. They've got skin in the game as well and oftentimes jealousies and animosities have built up because of the relationships they have with each other and from owning property together. The house and lot had been left to the surviving family from an uncle, Jake, who had no children of his own.

One of brothers said, "Uncle Jake said there would come a day when this property will no longer be owned together by family. I think today is that day." An inaudible sigh of relief, tinged with sadness, filled the room in that moment. As so many families do, unspoken assumptions have led to hard feelings and strained relationships. The good news is for this family, it's not too late. While the relationships are damaged, they are certainly not beyond repair.

I had done some previous consulting work with one of the brothers. When he saw the impasse that was coming because of the different needs and desires the brothers had, he offered to bring me in and pay for it himself in an effort to find middle ground. His brother agreed because he, too, was concerned about the relationship and the love they have for each other. Sometimes this type of help is absolutely necessary to work through testy issues.

For me and my personal situation with my father in our business, I had coaching for quite a while before I was able to confront my father with some of the issues we had. My old mentor, Arno, had helped me think through and develop a means of addressing Dad that he could hear and respond too, not with impatience and anger, but thoughtfully and with respect for my need and right to say what I was thinking.

During the third year of working with my father I'd had all the fun I could stand. The relationship sucked and the strain of working together had become almost too much for both of us. I wanted to go to seminary and get out of his world. Instead, after some intense help from the outside and some contemplation of what I would lose if I did that, I decided to have "the conversation"-- the conversation we all dread and therefore rarely risk.

I made an appointment with my father. We met in the back den of the house I'd grown up in. It was mid-afternoon on a warm spring day. When I started talking, I felt a flood of repressed emotion let go. I felt all the frustration unleash and I let him have it.

For an hour and a half I bombarded him with all the debris I had swept under the rug, not just for these 3 years but for all my 30 years. It was now or never and in the end I had nothing left to lose: if it didn't get better I would leave or get fired; if it got better I was ahead of the game.

Normally, Dad would have been brusque and discounting of me, but for some reason this time was different. He sat there, interrupting only one time when I said I was tired of being second guessed. He stopped me and said that part is not true. I've given you all the leeway you've needed to learn by making some mistakes, he said, and he was right. I realized that I had to stick to the facts of my feelings and not wander off into the bushes of accusation. That wouldn't accomplish anything worthwhile.

My preparation and moment of maturity worked. I'd never talked to my father like I did that day, nor did I ever again. That conversation was a success. It accomplished the purposes I had laid out it in my mind and my father and I developed a deeper, more authentic relationship from that day forward.

Taking the risk to speak up, to no longer be able to sweep my feelings aside and play like they didn't exist, made all the difference. The lump, while still present, was much smaller. Dad and I worked together very successfully for another 12 years until his death.

Ask yourself: is the short term discomfort of "the conversation" worth the potential freedom and life improvement of taking the risk? If the discomfort is too much and you don't speak up, you've made your choice, quit complaining. If you prepare yourself and take the risk the short term discomfort, you may just find a wealth of long term good as you emerge into a new way of life in your relationships with the significant others of your family and your business.

The Comb Over Effect

A photo of my father at about age 25 shows him pretty much bald, but very handsome. My own crop of dark, curly hair, always worn slightly longer than standard issue, began departing in my late 20's and continues today. I've always embraced the old adage that: God created a few perfect heads, the rest He covered with hair. Therefore, I have not been tempted at any time to comb over the growing bare patch.

One of my dear attorney friends had hair about a foot long on the left side of his head that was coiled with precision around his shiny pate. When I first noticed this intricate web I thought, who's this guy foolin'? The answer was obvious, himself; bless his heart.

So it is with leaders who have to know it all, but who have a bare patch of expertise, experience or knowledge in their repertoire. They're simply combing over the lack of knowledge or information and fooling only themselves. Everyone can see the uncertainty and the fear of not knowing arise in the leader's behavior under stress.

Generally speaking, trying to deny or hide a deficiency just exaggerates it and makes it even more obvious. Trying to conceal the truth that you don't know the answer or that you're denying a mistake leads to a perception that you're disingenuous, slightly deceptive or unaware of how your actions and words affect those around you.

Leaders simply can't afford to be regarded as untrustworthy or unaware. Too much rides on the ability of team members to trust each other and to be open to others' input for the leader to try to hide out behind behavior that is transparent anyway. Know-it-all leaders cannot build collaboration. They will spawn competitive or avoidant situations incapable of sustained, high level activity.

A collaborative work environment requires 3 things of its members:

- Each individual feels high self-regard and is concerned about his/her position as a member.
- Each person must have sufficient respect for the other members to make the effort worthwhile.
- Each individual must be concerned for the quality of the relationships.

To the degree team members care for their own interests, the interests of the others and the relationships, the team can function collaboratively. Collaboration is the management strategy most closely associated with positive outcomes. It can only be achieved when all parties are listening well and have suspended their need to defend their position.

Have you ever worked with someone who had to be right all the time? Could you ever feel you were valued by that person? Probably not so much.

How can someone committed to being right allow room for input or guidance from others? They can't.

Acknowledgment of fallibility would crack the delicate shell of perfection with which they must surround themselves. As the old therapy joke goes, "You can't recover from arrogance because you'll never ask for help!"

During times of succession and power transfer it is especially important for leaders to be open to input from key others. A need to be right will keep crucial information from flowing and cause a jamming of the process at the most inopportune times. Much too often I've seen the older generation stick to old patterns of having to know it all that leave no room for others' contributions.

If a younger generation is to come to power in a family business, father/mother can't know best all the time. There has to be room for the next in line to have direct, regular input into decision making, in fact, it is the only way a successful transfer can occur. Otherwise the younger people will not be prepared to take over leadership and it creates a situation where the elders can step right back in and overturn a succession under the guise that their successors cannot and will not get it right.

Tell Me a Story

> *Recent research by Joanne Martin and her team at Stanford Business School shows that illustrative stories told within an organization encourage more commitment, generate more belief, and are more often remembered than statistical data that proves the same point in a factual way.*
>
> *Stand in Your Power blog, Randy Siegel*

This was certainly my experience in my years of working with my father. Every workday that he and I were both in town began in someone's office at 8:15. My brother-in-law was there sometimes, the EVP was often there and Dad would begin by relating a story of how he and his "friendly competitors" had done what they'd done over the years.

Some of the stories were cautionary tales about what not to do. Other stories were about how he put together a syndicate of business people to buy, renovate and sell one textile mill after another. They were exciting stories, even though after years of hearing them, I knew the outcome. There was the drama of deals nearly failed because of the inability to put together the financing and how they were pulled out of the fire at the last moment.

There was another story he loved to tell about how a competitor went after him to put him out of business. This story entailed the other company buying a huge amount of quarterly production out from under Dad at above market prices, just at the top of the market. The commodity price plummeted and left the competitor having to buy material that was ultimately worth about 50% of what he was paying. One of Dad's friends told him later that the competitor looked out his window on a rainy day and said, "So, this is how you go broke in this business."

What a lesson for us all! The message was passed on to us in a much more powerful way than would have been possible with just the metrics of dollar and pound figures. We never forgot that our business lived and died on the "buy" side. If we got that part wrong it was a slippery and irrevocable slope toward failure.

Oftentimes in my work with family businesses I'll ask to hear some of the stories that are the genetic code of their enterprise. Generally one of the older members will recall something about their parents or relatives and how their influence created the culture that built the business. Such stories pass on the heritage of the family business and build commitment to it.

These stories hold real value for the younger members. They deepen relationships by reinforcing the shared experience from which the individuals emerge. They also help instill a belief that our predecessors persevered through difficult times and succeeded, and so can we.

Nurture storytelling in your company; it can be equally as powerful as sharing performance data, and will plant seeds for the future. What you do today is part of the story that will remain after you're gone. Make it a story of hope and possibility.

The Get Rich and Stay Rich Equation

Recently I presented to a group of bankers from both the commercial lending and wealth management sides of a bank. The title of the talk was "Wealth: Creation, preservation and succession." My objective was to help these men and women think in terms of the "human side" of wealth that I've discussed here before. These particular bankers are intimately involved with high net worth individuals who own privately-held businesses in the areas of financing their companies, helping them achieve their goals and passing the wealth to the next generation.

I asked the bankers to think of these customers on a continuum from the earliest stages of starting a business to preserving their wealth through thick and thin, and holding it all together to pass to their successors. I called the continuum from being a "get rich" customer to a "stay rich" customer. In these difficult economic times holding on to what one has created is tough.

- The "get rich" group's primary question might be, "How do I maximize earnings and retention for myself and my family?"
- The "stay rich" group's question might be, "How do I preserve the wealth I've created to pass to subsequent generations?"

As business founders/owners move from the get rich frame of mind to the stay rich way of thinking, some things happen. Primarily, while they get help in most areas of their business life in the forms of CPAs, attorneys, financial planners, insurance experts, etc., they most often fail to seek help in this human side where most good plans go bad.

Kids grow up and aren't so cute and cuddly anymore and they often show they lack the maturity, drive and initiative to carry on what they might be given. Also, the perks of wealth and ownership become more and more attractive and difficult to give up, so the desire to stay in power grows and the grip on power becomes irreversible.

There are 3 primary undesired outcomes of this "hold-on-till-you-can't-anymore" strategy:

- Tax and estate planning havoc
- Confusion and doubt among vendors, suppliers, employees, customers, bankers and other stakeholders
- Increase in sibling and relative rivalries as the doubt and confusion continue over time

So, what kind of help might a family get to deal with these potentially crippling issues? Some families use a family council that is privy to all the information and is used to make important decisions that affect the individuals and the business or wealth.

Others use an outside board of advisors to help give perspective. Still others might use a "family coach." The role of the coach is to help reach clarity about objectives. Once those objectives are identified the job then is to:

- Help establish a process for transfer—the "human side" of the equation
- Keep the process moving
- Keep important issues on the table (even when there is great temptation to brush them aside)
- Keep people practicing what they preach

Whatever you, as the leader of a privately held company, choose, it's important to seek assistance in thinking through crucial issues. Then it's important to have someone to help you work through them over time. The mark of a successful family business is often succession. Without help succession too often goes very wrong to the dismay and disappointment of everyone concerned.

The Fifth Child

A retired banker friend was the executive director of a regional community foundation. The foundation is the recipient of bequests from people who want part of their estate or wealth to be used for charitable purposes. Recently a mutual friend of ours, a retired, widowed attorney, passed away leaving the bulk of his estate to his four adult children. I'm sure it was a sizeable estate from his long time law practice and from his influential and prosperous client base. As he was doing his estate planning he told my friend, "I've got 4 children and I want my charitable estate to be my fifth child." The concept of the fifth child as an inheritor is a compelling image.

While there was no family business to keep the family connected around the wealth, our attorney friend set up a trust account in the foundation which the children would run. This corpus doesn't belong to the children, but by establishing the fund he created a vehicle for them to remain connected and to learn to work together. Granting gifts to worthwhile causes upon which they must have substantial agreement is a great piece of legacy for a family; perhaps more valuable than the dollars.

Here is a connection for them that doesn't involve their own money, and it provides them a way to continue giving for the benefit of their community. It keeps them working together on a project of mutual interest. Many family wealth lawsuits come from those who feel disempowered. By giving voice and input to all family members about their family's legacy a real harmony has a chance to develop as the children age and work together. After all, isn't this one of the greatest gifts we can leave, an opportunity for growth and development of relationships among our children and grandchildren?

One of the presentations I do from time to time is called "The Human Side of Wealth Transfer." Part of the presentation is that so often a pool of family wealth or a family business is quickly dissipated in the next generation. It's estimated that 80%+ of wealth transfers are largely dissipated in the lifetime of the subsequent generation.

Our dear attorney friend had come up with a way for the family to keep in touch around a common project for years to come. The money is held in trust and managed by the foundation, but the earnings (in years when such things actually occur) will be helpful in this community hit hard by severe job losses and housing decline.

The real genius of this plan is that there isn't a business about which they can disagree and argue, only money from which they can make grants. The plan gives the children an opportunity to deepen their understanding of financial matters and to experience the satisfaction of watching their father's hard work pay off into the future.

If the inheritors get all the cash at once upon death of the grantor, there's a strong likelihood that some of the recipients are going to run through it like—well, you know the analogies that might apply here. That will leave them disgruntled and yelling "Foul!" Having responsibility around a pool of money they can't touch is a learning device for them that might just educate them to wiser ways of using the gifts they have been given.

Change and Hope

The individual is capable of both great compassion and great indifference. He has it within his means to nourish the former and outgrow the latter.

—Norman Cousins

During the 2008 political campaigns we heard the words "change" and "hope" used relentlessly and insistently. As many have said, the only constant is change, and hope is right next to love as the most life-giving value in our lives.

Running parallel to these words in the campaign was a very clear image of change; the very foundations of our economic system were changing as if in a ground-liquefying earthquake. A friend of mine lived in the Marina District of San Francisco during the great earthquake of 1989. He said that it felt like the ground had become liquid under his feet. And so it is with many of us now—the stability we'd come to know and take for granted is no longer a constant.

At the YMCA recently I overheard a fragment of conversation between two men. One, sitting on a stool, putting on his shoes said to the other buttoning his shirt, "You know, we'll look back on these times as exactly what was necessary at this time of the history of our country."

The speaker's smooth, dark skin and deep gray beard gave

him the look of an elder, a man of experience and intelligence. It was no accident I heard these words of encouragement and wisdom at precisely the right time. It struck me that I had a choice to make: Do I choose to experience the future with hope or with fear?

Where do we put our faith and hope in these times? What institutions or associations can we turn to as sources of strength and courage? I believe we ultimately must find hope within ourselves. Perhaps these times help us realize where real value lies, and perhaps these recent holidays have reinforced that for those of us fortunate enough to have close, loving family and friends. No one or nothing can help us better gain the perspective we need in times like these than through close relationships and community.

Over the years of working in our family business with my father I got to know him as a man, not just as father. Just as importantly, he got to know me as a man. We somewhat inadvertently helped each other gain perspective on life through our time together. I see this now with my two grown children, we have gotten to know each other as human beings, not just as our roles, and have helped each other gain perspective on the passage of time and the evolution of life.

There is something very hopeful in that transition! I am moved by the ways in which we are now able to encourage and acknowledge each other.

With them both over the holidays I realized that we are really here for each other in ways that cannot be replicated outside of the family system. We can have friends and mentors, teachers and inspirers, but when we connect with family as humans, not just as the roles we've played for one another, then we've tapped into a source of strength that will serve us well.

Let's have faith in the coming years that, indeed, this is a time of rebalancing, a realigning of the foundation on which we'll live. Let's pick ourselves up, dust ourselves off and get back to work. The younger generations will know another world, and is it not always so with each generation? They will know a somewhat different world, one they help create.

Let's have faith that it will be a better world and that we may continue to contribute along with them for years to come, providing support, resources and encouragement to the ongoing process.

Finally, let's have faith that we will emerge from these times wiser, kinder and more compassionate people. When we build our business or any endeavor from that platform all else will fall into place.

Spread the good word, not the negatives and complaints. Tell a different story than you hear around you. Uplift and encourage others. Let those around you hear an optimistic tale. A funny thing just might happen; you might be uplifted by your own words. Our world can use all the uplifted people we can muster to right now.

COMMUNICATION AND RELATIONSHIP

The Paradox of Business Partner Relationships

> *The Abilene paradox is a story in which a group of people collectively decide on a course of action that is counter to the preferences of any of the individuals in the group. It involves a common breakdown of group communication in which each member mistakenly believes that their own preferences are counter to the group's and, therefore, does not raise objections.*
>
> *Wikipedia*

The Abilene Paradox is a concept, a parable really, created by Jerry Harvey over 3 decades ago. In brief, it's the story of a family sitting comfortably on the porch of the family house one hot, dusty Texas afternoon. Someone suggests they take the 53 mile ride to Abilene to have dinner at a cafeteria.

Eventually they all agree to take the long, disagreeable ride to eat bad food. When they return 4 hours later and are talking, it turns out no one really wanted to go, but they went along to get along.

There are analogies here for business partners who bring in outside help to help them solve their interpersonal problems. Here is what an outside consultant might hear from contentious business partners:

1. "We need each other and in the past we've been pretty

close, but now (name the topic) is going on and it's tearing us apart."

2. "If you'll just focus on my partner and 'fix' him, this will be right back on track, everything will be okay."

3. "At some level I know I'm also responsible for some of what is happening, but he started it!" Neither wants to anger, belittle or bypass the other, so they've remained stuck in inaction.

4. Both are angry at the stalemate and blame the other for it to some degree. Finger pointing and bitter judgment block the way to resolution.

5. While both do care for each other, both feel distant or disconnected from the other at this time. While there may not be a fissure, there is a crack in the dike that either gets repaired or a flood of negativity ensues.

6. One or both expect the consultant to fix the other so things will be better. Advisors aren't magicians. They have to ask, "Are these people willing and able to work through these issues and move forward? If yes, there's a chance. If no, probably not so much. A temporary patch is all we can hope for. The next pressure point can fire it all right back up.

Recently I've worked with a family business controlled primarily by two brothers with ongoing advice and support of the founder.

Both brothers, at some point in their initial interviews said that if his brother could just be "fixed", all would be okay. I told them both that I couldn't "fix" anyone, only they could do that. Also, neither of the brothers was really able to see or take responsibility for their own role in the disruptive disagreements that were hurting morale and damaging the business' effectiveness.

The truth is, in any interpersonal relationship, both parties are responsible for every situation. Unless one or both can get past blame and judgment about the other, no progress can be made. Only open and honest dialogue will take you where you want to go.

Consider your own situation. What are the contentious issues going unattended? What situations from the past need to be aired for the good of the individuals and the business? How might an outside perspective help clarify and work through the tight spots and bring an openness where people have been shut down?

In my own family business I used a mentor to help me work through issues and our CPA sometimes counseled my father. We were full of blame and judgment of each other. We were mired in a downward spiral that was leading nowhere positive.

The help we both received from having this outside perspective was invaluable because it allowed us to move from contention to cooperation and to enjoy the fruits of our work together. The bottom line: If you aren't able to communicate your preferences, need and desires to your partner, you may wind up in Abilene when you really didn't want to go!

Six Things I Know About My Family Business

Several years ago an organizational consultant with whom I was working introduced me to an exercise called "Six Things I Know About Myself." The object of the exercise was to get a group of people, oftentimes who'd worked together for a while, thinking in a similar vein and then using the resulting answers to stimulate dialogue in the group. Not only was the subsequent dialogue often deeper and more substantial than any of the group members had ever experienced with each other, but occasionally the individuals learned something about themselves.

Over time I adapted the exercise for use with family business members in an audience or family meeting. The object here is to get family members thinking about specific areas of their business and their working relationships in an attempt to address issues that may have been under the rug and tripping people up for quite some time.

I would encourage you and your working partners to answer these and then share the answers in a meeting. If people are free to express themselves honestly and openly there may be several revelations that could be of help to the family and to the business.

Answer them quickly, not thinking too much about each one, trusting that you readily know the answers, similar to what

Malcolm Gladwell advocates in his book, *Blink*. You may be surprised at the issues and potential solutions that arise from the spontaneity.

1. The thing I find most rewarding about being part of my family business . . .

2. The thing I find most challenging about being part of my family business . . .

3. I think these are the three major issues facing my family business at this point in its history . . .

4. If resources (time, money, personnel, etc.) were not an issue, this is how I would deal with these issues . . .

5. If I were to seek help with one issue facing my family business at this time it would be the issue of . . .

6. If I don't deal with these issues, three years from now my family business will be . . .

Once all relevant business members, family and/or non-family key employees, have answered them, get together, preferably with a facilitator, and have each person respond to the questions. If there is fear of reprisal for the answers then there are larger problems in play than strategy or tactics. To the degree possible allow the answers to flow without blame or judgment, the future of your company may depend on it!

Use these questions and answers to assess your situation. Use them as a way of working ON your business instead of just working IN it all the time. This broader view of things can lead to new and better results as members have the chance to see how everyone is feeling and thinking about the future of the business. New ideas for dealing with opportunities and potential threats might emerge.

The Human Side of Wealth Transfer

Last year a large insurance and investment company invited me to travel around the country delivering a presentation to financial consultants I call, "The Human Side of Wealth Transfer". After one of the seminars an attendee stopped me in the hallway and said, "You know everyone in the room was listening to you talk, but they were all churning inside because many of them are dealing with this subject in their own lives, not just in their clients' lives."

During the next session I was much more aware of this dynamic. I'd been talking to prior audiences from the perspective of their consultant's brain, but really it was more delicate a matter than that since it deals with an issue that is up close and personal to them.

Many of these men and women have done very well for themselves, despite the recent downturn. Several of them spoke to me about situations with their own children. One man who obviously had spent a lot of time thinking about it said to me that passing money to his only daughter was very difficult because of the life she was living. From his perspective, and probably rightly so, he knew that whatever he gave his daughter was going to be money badly used, leading to an even unhappier life in her future.

As my father used to say about running a business, compensation is the hardest issue. So it often is in family wealth, bestowing unearned wealth of children or anyone not prepared for it is a heavy burden on both sides of the equation. Here is what I advocate for individuals with wealth to pass on:

Seek professional help as you think through the emotional, psychological and relational issues that arise, hand-in-hand, with the process. Find someone you can trust and who is experienced in coaching the preparation and execution of the transfer. An attorney or financial advisor, a psychologist or a member of the Family Firm Institute might be a good resource for your needs.

There are 4 primary things I suggest you seek in an advisor to help during the process:

- Someone to help develop a rational, workable transfer process that suits you,
- Someone to keep the process moving, even when you want to delay or postpone,
- Someone to keep important issues on the table; there will be a tendency to take them off,
- Someone to help keep you practicing what you preach, until you legitimately say you want to try another approach.

You wouldn't think of making a major legal, real estate or investment decision without professional help, and so it should be with wealth transfer. There is a substantial risk in making people too rich, too soon.

Realize that wealth transfer, and succession of any kind, is hopefully a process, not an event. Assets and wealth are transferred by design or by accident. Most of those done by accident are not very successful. Take the time and initiative to:

- Set goals and objectives of what you want to occur,
- Clarify the roles and responsibilities of heirs and advisors well in advance,
- Foster an atmosphere of trust and communication,
- Be open about your intentions and seek necessary input to create more desirable outcomes.

Most wealth transfers fail in the next generation. The money is dissipated, diluted or disappears for over 70% of these transfers within the life of the heirs. By doing the proper preparation you can increase the odds that yours will be among the minority that can provide security and stability for their family for years to come.

The Secrecy Time Bomb

At a recent Family Business Center meeting Ernesto Poza, who literally wrote the primary textbook used in the Wake Forest MBA family business class, made an interesting comment and one with which I heartily agree. He said that "secrecy is the great single enemy of family business continuity." It's a bomb that generally goes off at the time of succession.

This is something I've discussed with a number of my family business clients over the years and an issue I've seen blow up for business families more than a few times. What does Ernesto mean by this? What is so toxic about secrecy in your family business? From my experience there are 3 major reasons secrecy is such a problem in the context of family business.

- First, a culture of secrecy keeps important and necessary information from flowing throughout the organization. For instance, if family members who work in the business are not informed about the finances of the company, assumption takes over. Every dollar of revenue is assumed to be a dollar of profit to those who don't know any better. Lack of information about expenses, investment and future uses of funds limits access to vital statistics that can hamper growth. This can cause jealousy, resentment and poor decisions.

- Second, a culture of secrecy, where the CEO keeps all relevant information to him or herself, leads to feelings of mistrust and distrust that run both ways. No one is really sure what can be discussed or what questions can safely be asked. Once anyone feels mistrusted their level of commitment goes down. Isn't it true for you that if you don't feel trusted you shut down and don't want to participate anymore? If the founder/owner keeps his or her plans for succession secret, everyone lives in doubt about their future in the company.

- Third, excessive secrecy, while protecting proprietary information from competitors, limits the development of the next generation of leaders. Part of developing successors is to involve them in important decision making functions, sooner rather than later. When succession time rolls around uninformed next generation members are often caught off guard and haven't had time or incentive to prepare themselves for the rigors and demands of taking over leadership positions.

By sharing information on a regular basis and thoroughly exploring questions and concerns, family business members and key non-family employees feel more connected to the company, more empowered to make good decisions and more committed to doing a good job.

There, of course, need to be ground rules about what is done with shared information, but once a foundation of trust is built the bomb can be defused and become much less likely to explode at the least opportune time.

Find ways to share information with each other. Learn to trust. Teach the next generation that there is responsibility that comes with access to important information, but with that responsibility comes a higher level of performance that can benefit all involved.

Home for the Holidays:

3 steps to a more peaceful season

When I teach or do presentations now, I sometimes bring my guitar and perform a song of mine written when I first started working as a family business consultant. It's called *All in the Family* and talks about the often troubled relationships that are brought together under one roof during family holidays.

After the first few lines of the song, those who're in a family that owns a business, laugh at the lines that go:

The blood flowing through us is all just the same,

We can't stand each other, but we share a last name.

Many of the students and business owners I talk to have experience with family member relationships gone terribly wrong when the mix of blood and money come together. They know it's too true that, while we're related by blood, we see the darkest part of certain relatives when the money and family come together.

How do we interact with these people during the holidays? If we continue to deal with each other from these old, outdated stereotypical ideas and images we've held for perhaps decades, we're asking for trouble and a continuation of negative patterns. Of course, we know by now that we can't change others; spare the energy! All we do have is potential control over our own behavior.

Here are 3 things you can consider as you come together with family members during the upcoming holidays. Perhaps you can be a catalyst for helping reshape the days to their original meaning, "holy days":

1)   These are tense times for most of us. Recognize this and imagine yourself being an agent of peace in an anxious system.

It's important for all of us to understand how our words, attitudes and actions impact those around us. Even a brief study of emotional intelligence (EQ) from the works of Daniel Goleman and other researchers can help us improve in this area. Understanding how we come across to others can go a long way to making peace and creating a better atmosphere.

2)   We all want affirmation and affection.   Imagine yourself reaching out with love to someone with whom you've felt angry or frustrated emotions.

This is a tough one because hard feelings have had years to temper and become entrenched. Continuing to blame and judge a sibling or other relative for what happened perhaps decades ago, however, keeps the conflict in place and makes it impossible to move forward. Many a prosperous, excellent business has sunk because of holding on to hard feelings even after so many years.

3)   We've all made mistakes. Imagine yourself forgiving, or letting go of blame for someone for whom you hold a

grudge.

Some old hurts may not heal in this lifetime. Those have to be dealt with in the best way possible. If you're still blaming your mother or father at 50, you've just got to get over it. You're an adult; the blame game is not a valid excuse for negative attitudes or behaviors.

In my song I wrote, "We smile as greet one another, but things are not quite the way they appear." Make the appearance real this year. Rise above pettiness and vindictiveness and help make the world a little better place, and family a place where peace on earth, and in your family business, can begin to be found.

Don't Be Defined by the Pressures of the Time

When a call from a family business owner comes through to my cell phone on Sunday afternoon I can be pretty sure that circumstances are dire. Something's going on that has the business or the family, or both, in some degree of turmoil. So it was, a while ago, when I got just such a call.

The surviving co-founder of this business had just visited his only son who works for a branch of the business in another city. During the course of their visit the son made it clear that he wanted a title and some ownership, sooner rather than later. Dad had made it clear that this wasn't going to happen for a while yet, at least until the son had proven he was more committed and competent than he had shown thus far.

When everyone was fat and happy and there was plenty of money, this situation could be swept under the rug, but now that things aren't so good the situation was coming to a head. The father wanted me to help him negotiate this difficult and testy situation.

In another recent case, two brothers were at odds with each other about ownership and use of family property they jointly own. Visions of multiple generations of the family enjoying the property suddenly seemed in jeopardy. Everything had been fine until the economic downturn made their continued mutual ownership and maintenance of the property difficult, if not impossible. Income uncertainty, increased property taxes and hurt feelings have made this formerly loving relationship between brothers and their families a minefield of hidden agendas, blame and recrimination.

The pressures of the time exacerbate family business and family wealth issues. Minor annoyances and misgivings that have previously been ignored, suddenly become major stumbling blocks. Behaviors that used to be just aggravating are now points of serious contention. Relationships are now being defined by the economic turmoil and accompanying anxiety.

There are 3 strategies* I encourage my clients to use to help them survive and even thrive during difficult times and to prepare for a brighter future:

- *Work with one another for a proper understanding of the problem.* Don't hide out in difficult times; now is the time to be more proactive in defining issues and handling differences with business partners and family members, not less.

- *Exchange accurate information to solve the problem together.* No gaming allowed! Tell the truth about what's going on. Don't deny or exaggerate the current issues, the wellbeing of the family and its wealth could be at stake.

- *Bring all of our concerns out into the open so the issues can be resolved in the best way possible.* Have the difficult conversations. Meet together even when it's uncomfortable. Bring in a facilitator to help mediate, if necessary, and listen to each other with Dr. Covey's principle of "seek first to understand."

Don't allow family harmony to be ruined in the current circumstances. Times will get better and you really don't want to spoil something as precious as loving relationships because of a short term difficulty. There are answers out there. No problem arises without its solution arising also. Seek together to find solutions that will serve current and future generations.

*R.L. Sorensen, 1999

"If something happens to me. . ."

A banker friend told me about a family business customer of his. The founder/owner, now in his mid-70s, refuses to inform his family of his estate plans concerning the company. His children, two of whom work in the business, aren't sure who will succeed him, as their father puts it, "If something happens to me. . ." Sadly, for all us, it's not if, it's when.

This father goes to his attorney every two years and updates his plans as he has for the last 15 years, but so far, according to him it's just been a waste of his time and money; he's still alive and in charge.

It's hard to argue with success, and this hard-driving septuagenarian has certainly had that. He has taken the seed of an idea from 50 years ago and grown it into a substantial tree that continues to shed fruit in many directions. While there have been many attempts by family, advisors and bankers to get him to discuss his plans, father knows best, and he will not be convinced otherwise.

Keeping everyone in the dark is a strategy, but what are some of the results of this succession strategy? Here are 3 brief examples and 3 undesired outcomes:

3 brief, but true, case studies:

- Dad holds on so long that by the time he seriously considers succession the health of his 60 year old son had deteriorated to the point that he is incapable of running the business. The son ultimately dies before the father.

- In another case, the son's health remained intact, but the desire to take over the day-to-day operations of the business dwindled to the point of extinction. When Dad was gone, so was his motivation to keep the business in the family. He took his money and ran!

- In the third case, the second generation son ran things so long that the third generation children never attained meaningful positions in the company. Leadership in this case passed directly to the fourth generation and the grandchildren now run the business as their parents never did.

3 undesired outcomes:

- This "hold-on-till-you-can't-anymore" strategy can create tax and estate havoc when time is up. Conveying a closely-held company without jeopardizing its financial viability is a difficult task in the best of circumstances and exponentially more difficult when surrounded by secrecy.

- Stakeholders, including vendors, employees, customers, bankers and others have a vested interest in what will happen when leadership and/or ownership changes hands. A bank customer without a viable exit strategy for their business is an increasingly risky borrower.

- Finally, and perhaps most devastating in the long run, when the family is kept in the dark about their parents' plans, sibling rivalries tend to build and fester. A tension is often created in the family that erupts full-blown when it's time to settle affairs.

A few years ago I worked on a mediated settlement between a brother and a sister involved in a bitter and expensive lawsuit, and closing in on the court date. The dispute between the two began to escalate when Dad named the son to take charge of things upon his death. His daughter felt this was just a repetition and continuation of what had happened all her life. Since she hadn't had a chance to express her opinion before her father's death, she was going to try to change things afterwards.

The family had already spent a small fortune in legal fees, and they were just getting started! Had there been some attempt to involve all the family in the decision process earlier, not only a lot of money, but also some very bad blood could have been avoided.

Just like too much of a good thing becomes bad for us, so holding on too long without beginning a process of power sharing and transfer can be bad for the family business.

LEADERSHIP, GOVERNANCE AND MANAGEMENT

Three Keys for Developing Worthy Successors

I'll never forget the time many years ago when my father looked at me in that certain way and said, "I never intended for you not to have to work for a living." It was one of those life-changing, Zen-arrow-to-the-middle-of-the-sternum moments. The light came on for me that I probably wouldn't be retiring in the foreseeable future.

My father had seen what that type of life had done to too many young people. He had witnessed at close range the debilitating effects that an assured income and net worth had on some of the children of his friends and business associates, and he wasn't going to do that to me. While he had my best interest heart, it was disappointing to know that he wasn't going to make me rich!

Entitlement mentality is what it's called. It's a mindset that assumes I'm a special case and the laws of the universe don't apply to me. It took me a while to get it that I wasn't a special case and the laws that others live by are mine as well. The problem with the entitlement mentality is two sided: first, I never have to develop my potential because I don't really need it to survive well and secondly, those around me are going to resent me.

My self-esteem suffers from lack of need to achieve and my relationships suffer because of the position in which I find myself. The outcome is that I'm not the one Dad's going to entrust his hard won business to when he wants or needs to step aside. He'd rather sell it or let someone from the outside run it if I'm not perceived and experienced as responsible, competent and worthy of trust.

Preparing children to live contributing and responsible lives is one of the main needs of those in family business. Without it, as we've all seen, things tend to fall apart. As the Chinese proverb says about wealthy families, "From rice bowl to rice bowl in 3 generations."

To the degree the younger generation is pampered, sheltered and not held accountable, the enterprise and the family relationships will suffer.

Here are 3 things to consider and pass along to your children as you prepare future generations for your family business:

1. Children determine their interest in a family business around the dinner table hearing their parents express either excitement about the business, or hearing their complaints about all that is going wrong. Kids are smart. They'll make their decision pretty quickly if the latter is the conversation they hear.

2. Hold children accountable in small ways from an early age. Help them figure out how to earn and use money and to make wise decisions about it. Help them learn about investing, saving and giving on a small scale to build confidence that they can make good decisions as

the stakes get higher.

3. If you have adult children in the business already, involve them in important meetings and decisions. Solicit their input and listen to them. You may find them naïve or immature, but give them room to grow and encourage this growth by making them feel like they can contribute. It will provide you with teachable moments when you can pass along instruction in real time.

Ultimately we all want to feel we contribute and that we are worthy. Help create an atmosphere for your children and grandchildren where this growth and development can occur.

Three Possibilities of Family Business

In a recent client meeting the business owner said he'd read a good bit of the literature of family owned business but "most of it focuses on the problems and not the possibilities." So, let's focus on the possibility of working with family for a few minutes. Why have people continued to work with family members even when it doesn't involve all hands needed to pick cotton or run the blacksmith shop?

What are the possibilities of working with family? How can we learn to look at it in that way, rather than in light of the unhappiness and discomfort it might cause from time to time?

First, from the human perspective, when a parent and child work together there is the possibility of growing the relationship. My father and I could barely carry on a civil conversation with each other when I first went to work with him. It was very uncomfortable. But, he knew and I knew that there was something of value buried under the dysfunction that was worth trying to find and salvage. Over our 15 years together we became dear friends and I got to know him as a man, not just as some childhood image left over to haunt my adult dreams.

Second, from the business perspective, when there is trust among the family members who work together, there's a sense that you're watching each other's backs. Over the years many of my clients and friends who own businesses, including myself, have experienced embezzlement, theft and waste on the part of employees who felt no accountability or oversight. A strong network of family members can provide the sense that there is someone watching who's going to make sure the interests of the business are well cared for.

Third, there is the legacy perspective, the possibility of building something for the future of the family, a legacy that endures beyond the departure of the founding generation. At a certain age we tend to turn from trying to fulfill just our own personal wants and desires to thinking about our children and grandchildren's futures. Can we be of help? Can we provide a platform from which they can work?

My old mentor, Arno, always said we all need "a platform to work from." We need a place we can hang our hats and feel the possibility that this is ours, that we can build it and nurture it and make it something that just might benefit generations of our family to come. While there are no guarantees any business will survive for the long haul, experience has shown us that the corporate world no longer provides that promise of lifetime employment and security.

Having a family business can be quite a blessing for any family, but it requires a commitment to trust and communication, clarity of roles and responsibilities, and unity of goals and objectives. When these factors can come together for the wise and healthy family, the possibilities are unlimited.

Family Business during Difficult Times: leadership, passion and education

> *Education is not the piling on of learning, information, data, facts, skills or abilities - that's training or instruction - but is rather making visible what is hidden as a seed.*
>
> *Thomas Moore*

In October 2009 at the Family Firm Institute's Annual Meeting, a panel of family business experts from around the world convened. While this meeting had been scheduled for well over a year the economic turmoil at that time provided the opportunity to ask some questions about what family businesses need to survive and eventually thrive again during these times of economic uncertainty. Their findings are published in a white paper from FFI[1].

Three issues stuck out for me in the report, their thoughts on leadership, passion and education.

- **Leadership** refers to the fact that as family businesses are passed from generation to generation there is often a dilution of the dedication and decisiveness of the founder's generation. If the strength and determination of a strong leader is not there, the viability and effectiveness of the enterprise will suffer.

In my two decades of working with family businesses, unprepared next generation leadership has been one of the principle stumbling blocks I've found among my clients.

Most often the founders of these companies have been men and women from "the greatest generation." They grew up in a time when making your own way in life was the only option. The qualities they displayed to form and sustain their businesses were very different from their children's experience. Unless the senior generation feels the younger generation is capable of leading, transition is going to be difficult and likely will come only after some life event that makes it happen.

As I've said before, succession can happen by design or by accident. If it is delayed too long because of lack of conviction that the younger generation can run the company, it will happen by accident, and the outcome is even more doomed to be undesirable.

- **Passion** refers to the fire in the belly that must exist in the next leaders. If the younger generation members feel their thoughts and opinions carry no weight and have no value they'll lose passion for the business.

Too many rules about what they have to do to earn a spot in the business may dampen their enthusiasm. The panel challenges the old adage that anyone wishing to join the business must have worked outside the company prior to coming back.

Really good potential successors may find careers that are more rewarding than they might find at home. Also, the values they contract in the public work world may be at odds with those the family really wants to instill in the next generation of leaders.

I worked as a banker for 4 years before coming back to our business. I learned responsibility for my contribution, as I'd had to do at the bank. In a family business consequences of poor performance are often minor or nonexistent. This hurts morale and competitiveness.

- **Education** has to do with the ongoing education every individual connected with the enterprise should have. Here, too, there are 3 major areas:
  1. Each person should have some knowledge of the enterprise. What is it? What has it taken and what will it take to succeed? In order to protect my own interests and to contribute, I need to be knowledgeable about it.
  2. Each person should learn that they are here to help "nurture and protect" the enterprise, not take advantage of it. There is no room for those who would take unfair advantage of the enterprise or the family through a sense of entitlement.
  3. Each person should learn how to manage their personal behavior and emotions. How do my behaviors and interactions affect communication, emotional tone, and potential for conflict in the enterprise?

After about 3 years of working with my father I attended a 9-day Outward Bound course in the mountains of North Carolina. I returned with a sense of self-reliance and self-confidence that I'd been unable to find before. I had a new determination to be Dad's successor and over the next couple of years, I did just that.

Leadership, passion and ongoing education: 3 areas of primary importance for family businesses as we go through unprecedented economic, political and emotional times.

[1]*The Challenges and Opportunities of Family Business during Economic Crisis,* FFI Update, December 2008, Volume XXI, Number 12

Adding Value to All Our Customers

No matter what our line of work we all want to add value to our customers, it's why they do business with us and why our businesses exist. The amount of perceived value we add to any given situation determines what we can charge, our unique selling proposition and the likelihood that we will keep that customer away from competitors.

One of my friends who has done a great job of adding value to his customers over the years has been an ongoing resource for thought provoking insights for me. He has spent more time, energy and money on training and both personal and organizational development than about anyone I know, and it has paid off handsomely.

Ken has always been able to help me with my thinking about marketing and customer service when I've asked for his help. He told me recently that he has focused on adding value to customers. He figures that if customers feel they are receiving good value for their money, all else falls into place. Adding value, according to Ken, is composed of 3 seemingly simple, not necessarily easy ingredients. He calls them: Creativity, Relationship and Leadership.

- **Creativity** in this context means providing capability. My customer needs to accomplish something and she turns to me because she feels I can help her get it done. Providing capability means I need to be on top of my game, I need to be good at what I do and I need to have others who are willing to verify I can do it and have done it for them over the years. My capability needs to include resourcefulness, imagination and energy.

Oftentimes when I'm hired by a family owned business it is late in the game. They've tried every method they can imagine to make peace or find a better way to get along. They've used up all the imaginative ideas they could come up with and they're low on energy because the conflict has often worn them down.

Part of my job is to give them a sense that there is a calm spot in the storm and they are capable of finding more creative ways of dealing with things than they have thus far, if we can get buy in from the key players. Family business owners are usually pretty resourceful people. Tapping into that resourcefulness is a necessary part of the work I do.

- **Relationship**, as we're using it here, means providing confidence. My customers or clients need to feel that they can turn to me in times of need and that they will not be disappointed. Building relationship requires ongoing contact, getting my name out there, building a reputation as someone who is true to my word and who will deliver, whatever it takes.

Recently at the Wake Forest Family Business Center seminar, the current president of a 125 year old family business told us the story of his family and the business they've built starting out in England all those years ago. It was obvious during his presentation that over the 5 generations the owners of the company have built relationships with their customers that are second to none. When the customer needs a particular machine for a unique application, they know they can turn to these folks and they will deliver.

The longer I work with family business, including the one my father and I ran for many years, the more I'm convinced that business is about relationship, first and foremost, both inside the business and outside as well. If you can develop the key relationships to the point of eliminating doubt as to capability, reliability and commitment, you're far down the road to winning the game.

- **Leadership** means providing direction. Customers turn to us oftentimes because they are adrift. They have a problem or an issue and don't know where else to turn. If we've proven ourselves to them or to others who are willing to vouch for our capability, customers feel they can call on us for help and we'll be able to help them move toward their goals and objectives. People are hungry for leadership. We are all captivated in the presence of true leaders. They make us want to go for it and to give extra effort because we feel we will not be led astray.

Years ago when I started doing this work, I was having dinner with a psychologist from Chicago. What he said to me jolted me as much as anything I've ever heard in psychology, as obvious as it might seem. It's also a lesson we can use in many different aspects of our lives. He said, "In order to do this work (consulting to family businesses and closely-held companies) we have to have almost equal measures of self-confidence and self-questioning."

It struck me that I had been leading with my self-questioning! I felt I was a fraud to some degree because while I had experience and education, I wasn't sure I had insights and processes I could offer that might shift dynamics and make a difference in the work and family lives of these good people. What I've discovered, however, is that when I lead with my self-confidence, people respond positively. As I said, we all want some leadership in our lives when the way is unclear and the current reality is murky. To the degree we can provide that leadership in our area of expertise, the greater the value we provide.

Creativity, relationship, leadership. By focusing on these qualities we not only provide our customers with what they need and want, but we become better competitors as well.

Ordinary People, Extraordinary Results

> *Never judge your partner's shortcomings too harshly, if they didn't have them they would have found someone better than you!*
>
> *Peter Schutz*

Peter Schutz, former CEO of Porsche, spoke at a seminar I attended a few years ago. He made many good points worthy of consideration by family business owners and next generation leaders. One uncomfortable truth is that "Every manager has the organization he or she deserves." How do we ensure that the organization we have is one we want, not one we get by default?

One way, according to Schutz, is to be mindful and plan carefully the type of culture we create in our business. Organizational culture is often taken for granted in family business because it is generally a reflection of the founder's attitudes and interests. At their best, a powerful, positive culture is a prime differentiator. Peter Drucker has said it best, "My culture will eat your strategy for breakfast!"

Schutz suggests that corporate culture is the thing we can control and that rather than culture being what we **will do**, it is easier to understand and pass along when it is based on "Thou shalt not. . ." statements. Culture is what we are **not going to do** in our business. He suggested these three as examples of what we will not do in our corporate cultures:

1. We will never misrepresent our products/services to get the business. Successful, long term business is built on relationships, and solid, lasting relationships will never come about from lying to customers. Business owners are smart and they've been lied to by the best. They're wary of anyone who over promises and under delivers.

2. We will never make another person smaller to build ourselves up. We are family. We're all in this together. We don't talk negatively about your family members, competitors, employees or suppliers to anyone. We never really build ourselves up by tearing others down.

3. We will never discuss our issues in front of vendors, suppliers, employees or customers. I suggest instead that a family who works together create "One Voice." This is the way they portray themselves in the community. The family businesses that are consistent in their presentation to outsiders and insiders has the greatest chance of survival in the long term.

Keep the "thou shalt nots" simple and short. Do you want to be a member of this tribe, this family? Are you willing to live by the "thou shalt nots"? Schutz made the point that ultimately we are all ordinary people, but ordinary people with enthusiasm and passion can produce extraordinary results.

The extraordinary will emerge if employees, family or not, are nurtured in an environment that supports and encourages. We do this by nurturing the dreams and aspirations of the employees. "Managing is a nurturing job," Shutz said. "Hire character and teach skills, never the other way around."

We nurture, in part, by inclusion. We make timely and quality plans together. We talk about the plans, get input and take our time in a democratic environment. We implement the plans with the involvement of ordinary people who execute flawlessly, but implementation is an autocratic job: implement like a dictatorship.

Finally, make sure you create an excellent administrative system, an accurate and timely method of keeping score so you and your people know how you're doing at all times.

The importance of a healthy organizational culture is often little understood and neglected in family business, but according to a master of creating strong culture, Peter Schutz, it is a crucial piece of the puzzle for corporate success.

Four Critical Aspects of Family Business

Questions to Ponder

Recently I gave a presentation to a group of family business owners on the subject of "Four Critical Aspects of Family Business." The premise of the presentation is that most business owners spend most of their time driving the business and give little attention to other aspects of the business that can provide some nasty surprises if neglected. Michael Gerber, in his book *The E-Myth*, discusses this fact and says in addition to working **IN** the business, leaders must also work **ON** the business.

In my own business over the years we worked on the day-to-day matters of sales, supply, delivery, quality control, finance, personnel, and customer satisfaction. It's easy to make these the primary and sometimes only functions to which we pay attention.

Over the subsequent years I've learned that owners also need to give consideration to 4 other aspects: governance, succession, leadership development and relationship management. Let's look briefly at each of these topics so you can see what you're working **ON**, in addition to the necessary drivers of your business.

GOVERNANCE

- Entry rules—what are the requirements for family members who want to come into the business?

- Codes of conduct—how are family members expected to behave and perform if they are accepted? What are the penalties for those who do not perform?

- Board of Directors/Advisors—a key determinant of family business success can be one or two people from outside who can help give perspective and counsel.

- Family Council—is there a regular opportunity for family members, both employed in the business and not, to meet and express themselves? Those who have no voice or say so are often the source of litigation and upset.

- Ad hoc committees—to deal with important matters that arise from time to time.

- Exit strategies—long range planning about how to leave the business and to whom it will be left is crucial to a successful passing of the baton.

SUCCESSION

- Who will lead?—this should be known well in advance and thought through rigorously and professionally.

- Successor requirements—what is required of the next generation of leaders?

- Successor preparation—who will coach, mentor and prepare successors?

- Successor/Leader future relationship—what help will be needed to ensure this relationship is solid. If it is not, succession will likely fail!

- Leader's preparation for exit—does the retiring leader have interests to move toward? If not, interference and undermining of new leaders often occurs.

- Succession event—this marks the transition in a public way so there is no mistaking who will make decisions in the future. Succession is not a single event, it is the culmination of a long-term planning process.

LEADERSHIP DEVELOPMENT

Coaching and developing leaders doesn't happen by accident. Successors must be trained and developed just as they are in public corporations. This is often done in conjunction with a professional coach who leads a process of:

- Data gathering—how is the successor viewed by others? What are his/her strengths and development needs?

- Feedback—giving feedback about what the

successor does well and where the work needs to be focused.

- Development plan—what steps need to be assured for development?
- Mentoring/Coaching—what support and help will the successor receive?
- Action steps—what is the roadmap that leads to a fully prepared successor?
- Monitoring—how to ensure the steps are followed and well learned.

RELATIONSHIP MANAGEMENT

Create structures to deal with disputes, disagreements and misunderstandings in real time, otherwise havoc will often ensue:

- Structured dialogue—formalized conversations that are thoughtful and to the point.
- Facilitated conversations—if there is a difficult issue it is often wise to include a mutually respected third party to help with its discussion and resolution.
- Mediation—when things get really tough a structured mediation session may be necessary. This allows both parties to have their say without being cut off or intimidated into silence.
- Group meetings—regular meetings encourage openness and a normal process to ease the

discussion of difficult issues.

- Feedback sessions—every employee family member should be given feedback about performance and behavior, just as non-family employees are. Otherwise, resentment will grow and poor performance and behavior may continue.

- Crisis management—finally, if relationships come to a head and cannot be resolved through other means, who can you turn to for help? Oftentimes it needs to be a respected, neutral third party.

Think about these issues as you work ON your business. Where is your company proficient and where are you deficient? These issues will not go away; they tend to grow in complexity and difficulty if left unattended.

The Halloween Workplace

> *True freedom lies in the ability to pause between stimulus and response and choose differently.*
>
> *Rollo May*

Talking recently with the Human Resource Director of a very successful 3rd generation family business, he discussed how, under pressure, the CEO's behavior and body language conveys a threatening demeanor that "freezes people out" and "shuts them down." The CEO is a very smart, bottom line oriented guy who knows better, but seems to be unable to control this negative behavior when things aren't going his way. How many business leaders today are facing negative circumstances that cause similar response? The answer is most likely, a lot!

As I talk with family business owners and key non-family employees, I emphasize something I heard years ago and have applied in my work: *the higher you rise in an organization, the less useful feedback you get.* Family and non-family employees often become scared of being shut down or frozen out and become less and less likely to let you know how you're coming across to others. The antidote to this syndrome is self-awareness and self-regulation.

There is an inseparable connection between the mind and body. When you feel the impulse to lash out rising in you, take a moment and ask yourself, "Why am I doing this, again?" If you do that often enough you have a chance of beginning to regulate your behavior and find other, less toxic ways of dealing with negative or difficult events, circumstances or people.

There's a compelling body of research emerging that confirms what many of us have known for years: a workplace that is friendly, relaxed, supportive, and gives a degree of freedom and autonomy to employees is generally more productive than ones that are not. An autocratic, inflexible, tense workplace creates lower productivity, absenteeism, and poorer employee health.

As economic, political and social times become more difficult, employees are often frightened and frustrated enough without the increased burden of coming to work in a negative environment. As the business leader you will have to make difficult decisions, cutbacks, economic tradeoffs; there's just no way around it. You don't, however, have to make life even more miserable for your people.

The Chinese symbol for crisis is composed of two pictographs: danger and opportunity. While these are dangerous times for us in many ways, they are equally times of opportunity for those who are willing and able to make them so. Learning to gain awareness of your behavior and to regulate it in incremental steps can ultimately lead to a stronger organization that just might emerge from difficult times a leaner, stronger, more motivated entity than before.

It often takes help from outside the system to achieve the insights that can lead to self-awareness and self-regulation. A coach, a mentor, a trusted advisor, a board of advisors, even a minister or counselor can help.

You don't have to turn your company into a frightening place full of ghostly entities. Even in scary times there is the opportunity to create something that will come out on the other side stronger and better for the difficulty.

ABOUT THE AUTHOR

Robert P. Caldwell, Jr., M.A.
Babcock Family Business Fellow
Wake Forest University Schools of Business

As a businessman with over 35 years of experience, including 15 years in his family-owned textile business, Robert has written over 60 published articles and often speaks on the unique interactions of family systems and business dynamics. As a family business advisor he provides guidance to family-owned and closely-held companies in the areas of succession planning, leadership selection and development, corporate governance, organizational culture, and conflict management strategies.

Robert received his B.A. in Political Science and Business from Wake Forest University and an M.A. in Organizational Development/Psychology from Vermont College of Norwich University. Since 2001 he has been the Babcock Family Business Fellow in the Wake Forest University Schools of Business. He holds the highest volunteer awards given by both District and Council levels of the Boy Scouts of America and served for many years as a regional director of First Union National Bank.

In 1996 Robert founded Family Firm Resources, LLC and has advised and coached dozens of families who share a business or a pool of wealth. He lives in Charlotte, NC.

www.ingramcontent.com/pod-product-compliance
Lightning Source LLC
Chambersburg PA
CBHW060409190526
45169CB00002B/823